This Planner Belongs To:

_____

_____

Plantastic Press

2020

January

S	M	T	W	T	F	S
			1	2	3	4
5	6	7	8	9	10	11
12	13	14	15	16	17	18
19	20	21	22	23	24	25
26	27	28	29	30	31	

February

S	M	T	W	T	F	S
						1
2	3	4	5	6	7	8
9	10	11	12	13	14	15
16	17	18	19	20	21	22
23	24	25	26	27	28	29

March

S	M	T	W	T	F	S
1	2	3	4	5	6	7
8	9	10	11	12	13	14
15	16	17	18	19	20	21
22	23	24	25	26	27	28
29	30	31				

April

S	M	T	W	T	F	S
			1	2	3	4
5	6	7	8	9	10	11
12	13	14	15	16	17	18
19	20	21	22	23	24	25
26	27	28	29	30		

May

S	M	T	W	T	F	S
					1	2
3	4	5	6	7	8	9
10	11	12	13	14	15	16
17	18	19	20	21	22	23
24	25	26	27	28	29	30
31						

June

S	M	T	W	T	F	S
	1	2	3	4	5	6
7	8	9	10	11	12	13
14	15	16	17	18	19	20
21	22	23	24	25	26	27
28	29	30				

July

S	M	T	W	T	F	S
			1	2	3	4
5	6	7	8	9	10	11
12	13	14	15	16	17	18
19	20	21	22	23	24	25
26	27	28	29	30	31	

August

S	M	T	W	T	F	S
						1
2	3	4	5	6	7	8
9	10	11	12	13	14	15
16	17	18	19	20	21	22
23	24	25	26	27	28	29
30	31					

September

S	M	T	W	T	F	S
		1	2	3	4	5
6	7	8	9	10	11	12
13	14	15	16	17	18	19
20	21	22	23	24	25	26
27	28	29	30			

October

S	M	T	W	T	F	S
				1	2	3
4	5	6	7	8	9	10
11	12	13	14	15	16	17
18	19	20	21	22	23	24
25	26	27	28	29	30	31

November

S	M	T	W	T	F	S
1	2	3	4	5	6	7
8	9	10	11	12	13	14
15	16	17	18	19	20	21
22	23	24	25	26	27	28
29	30					

December

S	M	T	W	T	F	S
		1	2	3	4	5
6	7	8	9	10	11	12
13	14	15	16	17	18	19
20	21	22	23	24	25	26
27	28	29	30	31		

2021

January

S	M	T	W	T	F	S
					1	2
3	4	5	6	7	8	9
10	11	12	13	14	15	16
17	18	19	20	21	22	23
24	25	26	27	28	29	30
31						

February

S	M	T	W	T	F	S
	1	2	3	4	5	6
7	8	9	10	11	12	13
14	15	16	17	18	19	20
21	22	23	24	25	26	27
28						

March

S	M	T	W	T	F	S
	1	2	3	4	5	6
7	8	9	10	11	12	13
14	15	16	17	18	19	20
21	22	23	24	25	26	27
28	29	30	31			

April

S	M	T	W	T	F	S
				1	2	3
4	5	6	7	8	9	10
11	12	13	14	15	16	17
18	19	20	21	22	23	24
25	26	27	28	29	30	

May

S	M	T	W	T	F	S
						1
2	3	4	5	6	7	8
9	10	11	12	13	14	15
16	17	18	19	20	21	22
23	24	25	26	27	28	29
30	31					

June

S	M	T	W	T	F	S
		1	2	3	4	5
6	7	8	9	10	11	12
13	14	15	16	17	18	19
20	21	22	23	24	25	26
27	28	29	30			

July

S	M	T	W	T	F	S
				1	2	3
4	5	6	7	8	9	10
11	12	13	14	15	16	17
18	19	20	21	22	23	24
25	26	27	28	29	30	31

August

S	M	T	W	T	F	S
1	2	3	4	5	6	7
8	9	10	11	12	13	14
15	16	17	18	19	20	21
22	23	24	25	26	27	28
29	30	31				

September

S	M	T	W	T	F	S
			1	2	3	4
5	6	7	8	9	10	11
12	13	14	15	16	17	18
19	20	21	22	23	24	25
26	27	28	29	30		

October

S	M	T	W	T	F	S
					1	2
3	4	5	6	7	8	9
10	11	12	13	14	15	16
17	18	19	20	21	22	23
24	25	26	27	28	29	30
31						

November

S	M	T	W	T	F	S
	1	2	3	4	5	6
7	8	9	10	11	12	13
14	15	16	17	18	19	20
21	22	23	24	25	26	27
28	29	30				

December

S	M	T	W	T	F	S
			1	2	3	4
5	6	7	8	9	10	11
12	13	14	15	16	17	18
19	20	21	22	23	24	25
26	27	28	29	30	31	

December

12/30/19 to 01/05/20

○ 30. MONDAY

PRIORITIES

○ 31. TUESDAY

○ 1. WEDNESDAY

TO DO

○ 2. THURSDAY

○ 3. FRIDAY

○ 4. SATURDAY / 5. SUNDAY

January

○ 6. MONDAY

PRIORITIES

○ 7. TUESDAY

○ 8. WEDNESDAY

TO DO

○ 9. THURSDAY

○ 10. FRIDAY

○ 11. SATURDAY / 12. SUNDAY

January

Week 3   01/13/20 to 01/19/20

○ 13. MONDAY

PRIORITIES

○ 14. TUESDAY

○ 15. WEDNESDAY

TO DO

○ 16. THURSDAY

○ 17. FRIDAY

○ 18. SATURDAY / 19. SUNDAY

January

01/20/20 to 01/26/20

○ 20. MONDAY

PRIORITIES

○ 21. TUESDAY

○ 22. WEDNESDAY

TO DO

○ 23. THURSDAY

○ 24. FRIDAY

○ 25. SATURDAY / 26. SUNDAY

January

○ 27. MONDAY

PRIORITIES

○ 28. TUESDAY

○ 29. WEDNESDAY

TO DO

○ 30. THURSDAY

○ 31. FRIDAY

○ 1. SATURDAY / 2. SUNDAY

February

Week 6

02/03/20 to 02/09/20

○ 3. MONDAY

PRIORITIES

○ 4. TUESDAY

○ 5. WEDNESDAY

TO DO

○ 6. THURSDAY

○ 7. FRIDAY

○ 8. SATURDAY / 9. SUNDAY

February

○ 10. MONDAY

PRIORITIES

○ 11. TUESDAY

○ 12. WEDNESDAY

TO DO

○ 13. THURSDAY

○ 14. FRIDAY

○ 15. SATURDAY / 16. SUNDAY

February

○ 17. MONDAY

PRIORITIES

_____

_____

_____

○ 18. TUESDAY

_____

_____

_____

_____

_____

○ 19. WEDNESDAY

TO DO

_____

_____

○ 20. THURSDAY

_____

_____

_____

_____

_____

○ 21. FRIDAY

_____

_____

_____

_____

_____

○ 22. SATURDAY / 23. SUNDAY

_____

_____

_____

_____

February

○ 24. MONDAY

PRIORITIES

○ 25. TUESDAY

○ 26. WEDNESDAY

TO DO

○ 27. THURSDAY

○ 28. FRIDAY

○ 29. SATURDAY / 1. SUNDAY

March

03/02/20 to 03/08/20

○ 2. MONDAY

PRIORITIES

_____

_____

_____

_____

_____

_____

_____

○ 3. TUESDAY

○ 4. WEDNESDAY

TO DO

_____

_____

_____

_____

_____

○ 5. THURSDAY

_____

_____

_____

_____

_____

○ 6. FRIDAY

_____

_____

_____

_____

_____

_____

○ 7. SATURDAY / 8. SUNDAY

_____

_____

_____

_____

_____

March

Week 11   03/09/20 to 03/15/20

○ 9. MONDAY

○ 10. TUESDAY

○ 11. WEDNESDAY

TO DO

○ 12. THURSDAY

○ 13. FRIDAY

○ 14. SATURDAY / 15. SUNDAY

March

03/16/20 to 03/22/20

○ 16. MONDAY

PRIORITIES

_____

_____

_____

_____

_____

_____

_____

○ 17. TUESDAY

○ 18. WEDNESDAY

TO DO

_____

_____

_____

_____

○ 19. THURSDAY

_____

_____

_____

_____

○ 20. FRIDAY

_____

_____

_____

_____

○ 21. SATURDAY / 22. SUNDAY

_____

_____

_____

_____

_____

March

○ 23. MONDAY

PRIORITIES

○ 24. TUESDAY

○ 25. WEDNESDAY

TO DO

○ 26. THURSDAY

○ 27. FRIDAY

○ 28. SATURDAY / 29. SUNDAY

March

○ 30. MONDAY

PRIORITIES

○ 31. TUESDAY

○ 1. WEDNESDAY

TO DO

○ 2. THURSDAY

○ 3. FRIDAY

○ 4. SATURDAY / 5. SUNDAY

April

Week 15

04/06/20 to 04/12/20

○ 6. MONDAY

○ 7. TUESDAY

○ 8. WEDNESDAY

○ 9. THURSDAY

○ 10. FRIDAY

○ 11. SATURDAY / 12. SUNDAY

PRIORITIES

TO DO

April

Week 16

04/13/20 to 04/19/20

○ 13. MONDAY

PRIORITIES

○ 14. TUESDAY

○ 15. WEDNESDAY

TO DO

○ 16. THURSDAY

○ 17. FRIDAY

○ 18. SATURDAY / 19. SUNDAY

April

Week 17

04/20/20 to 04/26/20

○ 20. MONDAY

PRIORITIES

○ 21. TUESDAY

○ 22. WEDNESDAY

TO DO

○ 23. THURSDAY

○ 24. FRIDAY

○ 25. SATURDAY / 26. SUNDAY

April

Week 18

○ 27. MONDAY

PRIORITIES

_____
_____
_____
_____
_____
_____
_____

○ 28. TUESDAY

○ 29. WEDNESDAY

TO DO

_____
_____
_____
_____
_____
_____
_____
_____

○ 30. THURSDAY

_____
_____
_____
_____

○ 1. FRIDAY

_____
_____
_____
_____

○ 2. SATURDAY / 3. SUNDAY

_____
_____
_____
_____

May

Week 19

05/04/20 to 05/10/20

○ 4. MONDAY

PRIORITIES

○ 5. TUESDAY

○ 6. WEDNESDAY

TO DO

○ 7. THURSDAY

○ 8. FRIDAY

○ 9. SATURDAY / 10. SUNDAY

May

Week 20

05/11/20 to 05/17/20

○ 11. MONDAY

PRIORITIES

○ 12. TUESDAY

○ 13. WEDNESDAY

TO DO

○ 14. THURSDAY

○ 15. FRIDAY

○ 16. SATURDAY / 17. SUNDAY

May

05/18/20 to 05/24/20

○ 18. MONDAY

PRIORITIES

○ 19. TUESDAY

○ 20. WEDNESDAY

TO DO

○ 21. THURSDAY

○ 22. FRIDAY

○ 23. SATURDAY / 24. SUNDAY

May

○ 25. MONDAY

PRIORITIES

○ 26. TUESDAY

○ 27. WEDNESDAY

TO DO

○ 28. THURSDAY

○ 29. FRIDAY

○ 30. SATURDAY / 31. SUNDAY

June

Week 23   06/01/20 to 06/07/20

○ 1. MONDAY

                                             PRIORITIES

○ 2. TUESDAY

○ 3. WEDNESDAY

                                             TO DO

○ 4. THURSDAY

○ 5. FRIDAY

○ 6. SATURDAY / 7. SUNDAY

June

○ 8. MONDAY

PRIORITIES

○ 9. TUESDAY

○ 10. WEDNESDAY

TO DO

○ 11. THURSDAY

○ 12. FRIDAY

○ 13. SATURDAY / 14. SUNDAY

June

Week 25

06/15/20 to 06/21/20

○ 15. MONDAY

PRIORITIES

○ 16. TUESDAY

○ 17. WEDNESDAY

TO DO

○ 18. THURSDAY

○ 19. FRIDAY

○ 20. SATURDAY / 21. SUNDAY

June

Week 26

○ 22. MONDAY

PRIORITIES

○ 23. TUESDAY

○ 24. WEDNESDAY

TO DO

○ 25. THURSDAY

○ 26. FRIDAY

○ 27. SATURDAY / 28. SUNDAY

June

○ 29. MONDAY

PRIORITIES

○ 30. TUESDAY

○ 1. WEDNESDAY

TO DO

○ 2. THURSDAY

○ 3. FRIDAY

○ 4. SATURDAY / 5. SUNDAY

July

Week 28

07/06/20 to 07/12/20

○ 6. MONDAY

PRIORITIES

_____
_____
_____
_____
_____
_____

○ 7. TUESDAY

_____
_____
_____

○ 8. WEDNESDAY

TO DO

_____
_____
_____

○ 9. THURSDAY

_____
_____
_____
_____
_____

○ 10. FRIDAY

_____
_____
_____
_____
_____

○ 11. SATURDAY / 12. SUNDAY

_____
_____
_____
_____
_____

July

Week 29

07/13/20 to 07/19/20

○ 13. MONDAY

PRIORITIES

○ 14. TUESDAY

○ 15. WEDNESDAY

TO DO

○ 16. THURSDAY

○ 17. FRIDAY

○ 18. SATURDAY / 19. SUNDAY

July

Week 30

07/20/20 to 07/26/20

○ 20. MONDAY

PRIORITIES

○ 21. TUESDAY

○ 22. WEDNESDAY

TO DO

○ 23. THURSDAY

○ 24. FRIDAY

○ 25. SATURDAY / 26. SUNDAY

July

○ 27. MONDAY

PRIORITIES

○ 28. TUESDAY

○ 29. WEDNESDAY

TO DO

○ 30. THURSDAY

○ 31. FRIDAY

○ 1. SATURDAY / 2. SUNDAY

August

Week 32   08/03/20 to 08/09/20

○ 3. MONDAY

                                      PRIORITIES

○ 4. TUESDAY

○ 5. WEDNESDAY

                                      TO DO

○ 6. THURSDAY

○ 7. FRIDAY

○ 8. SATURDAY / 9. SUNDAY

August

○ 10. MONDAY

PRIORITIES

○ 11. TUESDAY

○ 12. WEDNESDAY

TO DO

○ 13. THURSDAY

○ 14. FRIDAY

○ 15. SATURDAY / 16. SUNDAY

August

○ 17. MONDAY

PRIORITIES

_____
_____
_____

○ 18. TUESDAY

_____
_____
_____
_____

○ 19. WEDNESDAY

TO DO

_____
_____

○ 20. THURSDAY

_____
_____
_____
_____
_____

○ 21. FRIDAY

_____
_____
_____
_____

○ 22. SATURDAY / 23. SUNDAY

_____
_____
_____
_____

August

08/24/20 to 08/30/20

○ 24. MONDAY

PRIORITIES

○ 25. TUESDAY

○ 26. WEDNESDAY

TO DO

○ 27. THURSDAY

○ 28. FRIDAY

○ 29. SATURDAY / 30. SUNDAY

August

08/31/20 to 09/06/20

○ 31. MONDAY

PRIORITIES

_____

_____

_____

○ 1. TUESDAY

_____

_____

_____

_____

○ 2. WEDNESDAY

TO DO

_____

○ 3. THURSDAY

_____

_____

_____

_____

_____

_____

○ 4. FRIDAY

_____

_____

_____

_____

○ 5. SATURDAY / 6. SUNDAY

_____

_____

_____

_____

September

○ 7. MONDAY

PRIORITIES

○ 8. TUESDAY

○ 9. WEDNESDAY

TO DO

○ 10. THURSDAY

○ 11. FRIDAY

○ 12. SATURDAY / 13. SUNDAY

September

09/14/20 to 09/20/20

○ 14. MONDAY

PRIORITIES

○ 15. TUESDAY

○ 16. WEDNESDAY

TO DO

○ 17. THURSDAY

○ 18. FRIDAY

○ 19. SATURDAY / 20. SUNDAY

September

○ 21. MONDAY

PRIORITIES

*art due ✓, finish magic squares, pg. 5

6:7 in math packet

Reading Fine, Fine

- questions

○ 22. TUESDAY

finish library assignment ✓

○ 23. WEDNESDAY

TO DO

new reading chart

*Library due, work on getting to know you

○ 24. THURSDAY

- Place value - nearpod
- PE Flip grid

music assignment

- music assignment
- Math Teams assignment
  ✓ Place value riddles
- Freckle

○ 25. FRIDAY

↓

○ 26. SATURDAY / 27. SUNDAY

September

○ 28. MONDAY

*Music due, library due

○ 29. TUESDAY

○ 30. WEDNESDAY

○ 1. THURSDAY

○ 2. FRIDAY

○ 3. SATURDAY / 4. SUNDAY

PRIORITIES

- library assign
- journey pg. 46-47

TO DO

October

10/05/20 to 10/11/20

○ 5. MONDAY

PRIORITIES

○ 6. TUESDAY

○ 7. WEDNESDAY

TO DO

○ 8. THURSDAY

○ 9. FRIDAY

○ 10. SATURDAY / 11. SUNDAY

October

○ 12. MONDAY

PRIORITIES

○ 13. TUESDAY

○ 14. WEDNESDAY

TO DO

○ 15. THURSDAY

○ 16. FRIDAY

○ 17. SATURDAY / 18. SUNDAY

October

○ 19. MONDAY

PRIORITIES

○ 20. TUESDAY

○ 21. WEDNESDAY

TO DO

○ 22. THURSDAY

○ 23. FRIDAY

○ 24. SATURDAY / 25. SUNDAY

October

Week 44   10/26/20 to 11/01/20

○ 26. MONDAY

PRIORITIES

○ 27. TUESDAY

○ 28. WEDNESDAY

TO DO

○ 29. THURSDAY

○ 30. FRIDAY

○ 31. SATURDAY / 1. SUNDAY

November

○ 2. MONDAY

PRIORITIES

○ 3. TUESDAY

○ 4. WEDNESDAY

TO DO

○ 5. THURSDAY

○ 6. FRIDAY

○ 7. SATURDAY / 8. SUNDAY

November

Week 46   11/09/20 to 11/15/20

○ 9. MONDAY

PRIORITIES

○ 10. TUESDAY

○ 11. WEDNESDAY

TO DO

○ 12. THURSDAY

○ 13. FRIDAY

○ 14. SATURDAY / 15. SUNDAY

November

11/16/20 to 11/22/20

○ 16. MONDAY

PRIORITIES

○ 17. TUESDAY

○ 18. WEDNESDAY

TO DO

○ 19. THURSDAY

○ 20. FRIDAY

○ 21. SATURDAY / 22. SUNDAY

November

○ 23. MONDAY

PRIORITIES

○ 24. TUESDAY

○ 25. WEDNESDAY

TO DO

○ 26. THURSDAY

○ 27. FRIDAY

○ 28. SATURDAY / 29. SUNDAY

November

○ 30. MONDAY

PRIORITIES

○ 1. TUESDAY

○ 2. WEDNESDAY

TO DO

○ 3. THURSDAY

○ 4. FRIDAY

○ 5. SATURDAY / 6. SUNDAY

December

○ 7. MONDAY

PRIORITIES

○ 8. TUESDAY

○ 9. WEDNESDAY

TO DO

○ 10. THURSDAY

○ 11. FRIDAY

○ 12. SATURDAY / 13. SUNDAY

December

○ 14. MONDAY

PRIORITIES

○ 15. TUESDAY

○ 16. WEDNESDAY

TO DO

○ 17. THURSDAY

○ 18. FRIDAY

○ 19. SATURDAY / 20. SUNDAY

December

○ 21. MONDAY

PRIORITIES

_____

_____

_____

○ 22. TUESDAY

_____

_____

_____

_____

○ 23. WEDNESDAY

TO DO

_____

_____

○ 24. THURSDAY

_____

_____

_____

_____

○ 25. FRIDAY

_____

_____

_____

_____

_____

○ 26. SATURDAY / 27. SUNDAY

_____

_____

_____

_____

December

○ 28. MONDAY

PRIORITIES

○ 29. TUESDAY

○ 30. WEDNESDAY

TO DO

○ 31. THURSDAY

○ 1. FRIDAY

○ 2. SATURDAY / 3. SUNDAY

January

○ 4. MONDAY

PRIORITIES

○ 5. TUESDAY

○ 6. WEDNESDAY

TO DO

○ 7. THURSDAY

○ 8. FRIDAY

○ 9. SATURDAY / 10. SUNDAY

January

01/11/21 to 01/17/21

○ 11. MONDAY

PRIORITIES

○ 12. TUESDAY

○ 13. WEDNESDAY

TO DO

○ 14. THURSDAY

○ 15. FRIDAY

○ 16. SATURDAY / 17. SUNDAY

January

○ 18. MONDAY

PRIORITIES

○ 19. TUESDAY

○ 20. WEDNESDAY

TO DO

○ 21. THURSDAY

○ 22. FRIDAY

○ 23. SATURDAY / 24. SUNDAY

January

○ 25. MONDAY

PRIORITIES

○ 26. TUESDAY

○ 27. WEDNESDAY

TO DO

○ 28. THURSDAY

○ 29. FRIDAY

○ 30. SATURDAY / 31. SUNDAY

February

○ 1. MONDAY

PRIORITIES

○ 2. TUESDAY

○ 3. WEDNESDAY

TO DO

○ 4. THURSDAY

○ 5. FRIDAY

○ 6. SATURDAY / 7. SUNDAY

February

○ 8. MONDAY

PRIORITIES

○ 9. TUESDAY

○ 10. WEDNESDAY

TO DO

○ 11. THURSDAY

○ 12. FRIDAY

○ 13. SATURDAY / 14. SUNDAY

February

○ 15. MONDAY

PRIORITIES

○ 16. TUESDAY

○ 17. WEDNESDAY

TO DO

○ 18. THURSDAY

○ 19. FRIDAY

○ 20. SATURDAY / 21. SUNDAY

February

02/22/21 to 02/28/21

○ 22. MONDAY

PRIORITIES

○ 23. TUESDAY

○ 24. WEDNESDAY

TO DO

○ 25. THURSDAY

○ 26. FRIDAY

○ 27. SATURDAY / 28. SUNDAY

March

○ 1. MONDAY

PRIORITIES

_____

_____

_____

_____

○ 2. TUESDAY

_____

_____

_____

_____

○ 3. WEDNESDAY

TO DO

_____

_____

_____

○ 4. THURSDAY

_____

_____

_____

_____

_____

○ 5. FRIDAY

_____

_____

_____

_____

○ 6. SATURDAY / 7. SUNDAY

_____

_____

_____

_____

March

Week 10   03/08/21 to 03/14/21

○ 8. MONDAY

PRIORITIES

○ 9. TUESDAY

○ 10. WEDNESDAY

TO DO

○ 11. THURSDAY

○ 12. FRIDAY

○ 13. SATURDAY / 14. SUNDAY

March

○ 15. MONDAY

PRIORITIES

○ 16. TUESDAY

○ 17. WEDNESDAY

TO DO

○ 18. THURSDAY

○ 19. FRIDAY

○ 20. SATURDAY / 21. SUNDAY

March

03/22/21 to 03/28/21

○ 22. MONDAY

PRIORITIES

○ 23. TUESDAY

○ 24. WEDNESDAY

TO DO

○ 25. THURSDAY

○ 26. FRIDAY

○ 27. SATURDAY / 28. SUNDAY

March

○ 29. MONDAY

PRIORITIES

○ 30. TUESDAY

○ 31. WEDNESDAY

TO DO

○ 1. THURSDAY

○ 2. FRIDAY

○ 3. SATURDAY / 4. SUNDAY

April

04/05/21 to 04/11/21

○ 5. MONDAY

PRIORITIES

○ 6. TUESDAY

○ 7. WEDNESDAY

TO DO

○ 8. THURSDAY

○ 9. FRIDAY

○ 10. SATURDAY / 11. SUNDAY

April

Week 15

04/12/21 to 04/18/21

○ 12. MONDAY

PRIORITIES

_____

_____

_____

○ 13. TUESDAY

_____

_____

_____

_____

○ 14. WEDNESDAY

TO DO

_____

_____

○ 15. THURSDAY

_____

_____

_____

_____

○ 16. FRIDAY

_____

_____

_____

_____

_____

○ 17. SATURDAY / 18. SUNDAY

_____

_____

_____

_____

April

○ 19. MONDAY

PRIORITIES

○ 20. TUESDAY

○ 21. WEDNESDAY

TO DO

○ 22. THURSDAY

○ 23. FRIDAY

○ 24. SATURDAY / 25. SUNDAY

April

○ 26. MONDAY

PRIORITIES

_____
_____
_____
_____
_____
_____

○ 27. TUESDAY

○ 28. WEDNESDAY

TO DO

_____
_____
_____
_____
_____

○ 29. THURSDAY

_____
_____
_____
_____

○ 30. FRIDAY

_____
_____
_____
_____

○ 1. SATURDAY / 2. SUNDAY

_____
_____
_____
_____

May

Week 18

05/03/21 to 05/09/21

○ 3. MONDAY

PRIORITIES

○ 4. TUESDAY

○ 5. WEDNESDAY

TO DO

○ 6. THURSDAY

○ 7. FRIDAY

○ 8. SATURDAY / 9. SUNDAY

May

05/10/21 to 05/16/21

○ 10. MONDAY

○ 11. TUESDAY

○ 12. WEDNESDAY

○ 13. THURSDAY

○ 14. FRIDAY

○ 15. SATURDAY / 16. SUNDAY

PRIORITIES

_____

_____

_____

_____

_____

_____

_____

TO DO

_____

_____

_____

_____

_____

_____

_____

_____

_____

_____

_____

_____

_____

May

○ 17. MONDAY

PRIORITIES

○ 18. TUESDAY

○ 19. WEDNESDAY

TO DO

○ 20. THURSDAY

○ 21. FRIDAY

○ 22. SATURDAY / 23. SUNDAY

May

05/24/21 to 05/30/21

○ 24. MONDAY

PRIORITIES

○ 25. TUESDAY

○ 26. WEDNESDAY

TO DO

○ 27. THURSDAY

○ 28. FRIDAY

○ 29. SATURDAY / 30. SUNDAY

May

05/31/21 to 06/06/21

○ 31. MONDAY

PRIORITIES

○ 1. TUESDAY

○ 2. WEDNESDAY

TO DO

○ 3. THURSDAY

○ 4. FRIDAY

○ 5. SATURDAY / 6. SUNDAY

June

Week 23

06/07/21 to 06/13/21

○ 7. MONDAY

PRIORITIES

_____

_____

_____

○ 8. TUESDAY

_____

_____

_____

_____

○ 9. WEDNESDAY

TO DO

_____

_____

○ 10. THURSDAY

_____

_____

_____

_____

○ 11. FRIDAY

_____

_____

_____

○ 12. SATURDAY / 13. SUNDAY

_____

_____

_____

June

Week 24   06/14/21 to 06/20/21

○ 14. MONDAY

                                PRIORITIES

○ 15. TUESDAY

○ 16. WEDNESDAY

                                TO DO

○ 17. THURSDAY

○ 18. FRIDAY

○ 19. SATURDAY / 20. SUNDAY

June

○ 21. MONDAY

PRIORITIES

_____

_____

_____

_____

○ 22. TUESDAY

_____

_____

_____

_____

○ 23. WEDNESDAY

TO DO

_____

_____

○ 24. THURSDAY

_____

_____

_____

_____

○ 25. FRIDAY

_____

_____

_____

_____

○ 26. SATURDAY / 27. SUNDAY

_____

_____

_____

_____

_____

June

Week 26   06/28/21 to 07/04/21

○ 28. MONDAY

PRIORITIES

○ 29. TUESDAY

○ 30. WEDNESDAY

TO DO

○ 1. THURSDAY

○ 2. FRIDAY

○ 3. SATURDAY / 4. SUNDAY

July

Week 27

07/05/21 to 07/11/21

○ 5. MONDAY

PRIORITIES

○ 6. TUESDAY

○ 7. WEDNESDAY

TO DO

○ 8. THURSDAY

○ 9. FRIDAY

○ 10. SATURDAY / 11. SUNDAY

July

07/12/21 to 07/18/21

○ 12. MONDAY

PRIORITIES

○ 13. TUESDAY

○ 14. WEDNESDAY

TO DO

○ 15. THURSDAY

○ 16. FRIDAY

○ 17. SATURDAY / 18. SUNDAY

July

○ 19. MONDAY

PRIORITIES

○ 20. TUESDAY

○ 21. WEDNESDAY

TO DO

○ 22. THURSDAY

○ 23. FRIDAY

○ 24. SATURDAY / 25. SUNDAY

July

Week 30

07/26/21 to 08/01/21

○ 26. MONDAY

PRIORITIES

○ 27. TUESDAY

○ 28. WEDNESDAY

TO DO

○ 29. THURSDAY

○ 30. FRIDAY

○ 31. SATURDAY / 1. SUNDAY

August

08/02/21 to 08/08/21

○ 2. MONDAY

PRIORITIES

○ 3. TUESDAY

○ 4. WEDNESDAY

TO DO

○ 5. THURSDAY

○ 6. FRIDAY

○ 7. SATURDAY / 8. SUNDAY

August

08/09/21 to 08/15/21

○ 9. MONDAY

PRIORITIES

○ 10. TUESDAY

○ 11. WEDNESDAY

TO DO

○ 12. THURSDAY

○ 13. FRIDAY

○ 14. SATURDAY / 15. SUNDAY

August

Week 33

08/16/21 to 08/22/21

◯ 16. MONDAY

PRIORITIES

◯ 17. TUESDAY

◯ 18. WEDNESDAY

TO DO

◯ 19. THURSDAY

◯ 20. FRIDAY

◯ 21. SATURDAY / 22. SUNDAY

August

Week 34

Week 34   08/23/21 to 08/29/21

○ 23. MONDAY

PRIORITIES

_____
_____

○ 24. TUESDAY

_____
_____
_____
_____
_____

○ 25. WEDNESDAY

TO DO

_____
_____

○ 26. THURSDAY

_____
_____
_____
_____
_____

○ 27. FRIDAY

_____
_____
_____
_____
_____

○ 28. SATURDAY / 29. SUNDAY

_____
_____
_____
_____

August

Week 35 08/30/21 to 09/05/21

○ 30. MONDAY

PRIORITIES

○ 31. TUESDAY

○ 1. WEDNESDAY

TO DO

○ 2. THURSDAY

○ 3. FRIDAY

○ 4. SATURDAY / 5. SUNDAY

September

○ 6. MONDAY

PRIORITIES

○ 7. TUESDAY

○ 8. WEDNESDAY

TO DO

○ 9. THURSDAY

○ 10. FRIDAY

○ 11. SATURDAY / 12. SUNDAY

September

○ 13. MONDAY

PRIORITIES

○ 14. TUESDAY

○ 15. WEDNESDAY

TO DO

○ 16. THURSDAY

○ 17. FRIDAY

○ 18. SATURDAY / 19. SUNDAY

September

09/20/21 to 09/26/21

○ 20. MONDAY

PRIORITIES

○ 21. TUESDAY

○ 22. WEDNESDAY

TO DO

○ 23. THURSDAY

○ 24. FRIDAY

○ 25. SATURDAY / 26. SUNDAY

September

○ 27. MONDAY

PRIORITIES

○ 28. TUESDAY

○ 29. WEDNESDAY

TO DO

○ 30. THURSDAY

○ 1. FRIDAY

○ 2. SATURDAY / 3. SUNDAY

October

○ 4. MONDAY

PRIORITIES

○ 5. TUESDAY

○ 6. WEDNESDAY

TO DO

○ 7. THURSDAY

○ 8. FRIDAY

○ 9. SATURDAY / 10. SUNDAY

October

Week 41   10/11/21 to 10/17/21

○ 11. MONDAY

PRIORITIES

○ 12. TUESDAY

○ 13. WEDNESDAY

TO DO

○ 14. THURSDAY

○ 15. FRIDAY

○ 16. SATURDAY / 17. SUNDAY

October

10/18/21 to 10/24/21

○ 18. MONDAY

PRIORITIES

○ 19. TUESDAY

○ 20. WEDNESDAY

TO DO

○ 21. THURSDAY

○ 22. FRIDAY

○ 23. SATURDAY / 24. SUNDAY

October

Week 43

10/25/21 to 10/31/21

○ 25. MONDAY

PRIORITIES

○ 26. TUESDAY

○ 27. WEDNESDAY

TO DO

○ 28. THURSDAY

○ 29. FRIDAY

○ 30. SATURDAY / 31. SUNDAY

November

Week 44   11/01/21 to 11/07/21

○ 1. MONDAY

PRIORITIES

○ 2. TUESDAY

○ 3. WEDNESDAY

TO DO

○ 4. THURSDAY

○ 5. FRIDAY

○ 6. SATURDAY / 7. SUNDAY

November

11/08/21 to 11/14/21

○ 8. MONDAY

PRIORITIES

○ 9. TUESDAY

○ 10. WEDNESDAY

TO DO

○ 11. THURSDAY

○ 12. FRIDAY

○ 13. SATURDAY / 14. SUNDAY

November

○ 15. MONDAY

PRIORITIES

○ 16. TUESDAY

○ 17. WEDNESDAY

TO DO

○ 18. THURSDAY

○ 19. FRIDAY

○ 20. SATURDAY / 21. SUNDAY

November

11/22/21 to 11/28/21

○ 22. MONDAY

PRIORITIES

_____

_____

_____

○ 23. TUESDAY

_____

_____

_____

_____

_____

○ 24. WEDNESDAY

TO DO

_____

_____

○ 25. THURSDAY

_____

_____

_____

_____

○ 26. FRIDAY

_____

_____

_____

_____

_____

○ 27. SATURDAY / 28. SUNDAY

_____

_____

_____

_____

November

11/29/21 to 12/05/21

○ 29. MONDAY

PRIORITIES

○ 30. TUESDAY

○ 1. WEDNESDAY

TO DO

○ 2. THURSDAY

○ 3. FRIDAY

○ 4. SATURDAY / 5. SUNDAY

December

○ 6. MONDAY

PRIORITIES

_____

_____

○ 7. TUESDAY

_____

_____

_____

_____

_____

○ 8. WEDNESDAY

TO DO

_____

_____

○ 9. THURSDAY

_____

_____

_____

_____

_____

○ 10. FRIDAY

_____

_____

_____

_____

_____

○ 11. SATURDAY / 12. SUNDAY

_____

_____

_____

_____

December

12/13/21 to 12/19/21

○ 13. MONDAY

PRIORITIES

○ 14. TUESDAY

○ 15. WEDNESDAY

TO DO

○ 16. THURSDAY

○ 17. FRIDAY

○ 18. SATURDAY / 19. SUNDAY

December

12/20/21 to 12/26/21

○ 20. MONDAY

PRIORITIES

_____

_____

_____

○ 21. TUESDAY

_____

_____

_____

_____

○ 22. WEDNESDAY

TO DO

_____

_____

○ 23. THURSDAY

_____

_____

_____

_____

_____

○ 24. FRIDAY

_____

_____

_____

_____

_____

○ 25. SATURDAY / 26. SUNDAY

_____

_____

_____

_____

December

○ 27. MONDAY

PRIORITIES

○ 28. TUESDAY

○ 29. WEDNESDAY

TO DO

○ 30. THURSDAY

○ 31. FRIDAY

○ 1. SATURDAY / 2. SUNDAY

Made in the USA
Monee, IL
05 September 2020